ROMAN LIfE
AT THE YORKSHIRE MUSEUM

GALLERY GUIDE

THE ROMANS ARRIVE
Conquest of the North

The Romans invaded Britain in AD43. An army of about 40,000 men, led by Aulus Plautius, landed on the Kentish coast and won a battle against the British at the River Medway before advancing to the River Thames near London. The four legions, named II Augusta, IX Hispana, XIV Gemina, and XX Valeria, with accompanying auxiliary troops, awaited the arrival of the Emperor Claudius before marching on Camulodunum (Colchester), the centre of the Catuvellauni. There the tribal leaders who had been defeated in battle submitted to the Romans and others, who wished to be Roman allies, negotiated peaceful settlements.

One of the British leaders who may have signed a treaty with Rome at that time was Queen Cartimandua, leader of the principal tribe of northern England known as the Brigantes. They were certainly Roman allies before 50. Cartimandua herself was described by the historian Tacitus as being 'from a powerful family.' It was not until 69, when Cartimandua lost her power to her rebellious

The movements of the legions during the conquest of southern Britain and Brigantia

Decorated silvered bronzes from cavalry harness, Fremington Hagg, Swaledale

ex-husband Venutius, that the treaty was broken. As stated by Tacitus 'Venutius had the Kingdom while we had a war to fight.'

In 71 Q. Petillius Cerialis led the 9th legion into the North to subdue Venutius and to add his kingdom to the province of Britain. The army moved into east Yorkshire and after founding a legionary site at York headed northwards, crossing the Pennines towards Carlisle over the Stainmore pass. Archaeological evidence is not available for the fierce battles recorded by Tacitus. However, the major Brigantian stronghold at Stanwick was abandoned about this time and it is likely that one of the battles was in its vicinity. The route of the army is evident from the remains of temporary camps constructed by the legionaries on their march over the Pennines.

The commander Cerialis had virtually conquered the Brigantes but did not have time to consolidate his gains before his recall to Rome. It was not until Agricola was governor c.80 that the network of military roads and forts was constructed over Brigantia as a whole.

Tombstone from York of L Duccius Rufinus, standard bearer of the 9th Legion

The extent of the Empire in AD 43 showing the previous fortresses of the legions which came to Britain

THE BRIGANTES
Tribal society in the North

Little is known about the Brigantes and their way of life. They were a tribal society in which the aristocratic elite had power and wealth, and the majority of the people were poor. Archaeological evidence has shown that most lived a very basic existence on small farmsteads. They were mainly pastoralists, though they would have grown cereal crops as well. Thousands of their farmsteads have been spotted on aerial photographs. Several have recently been discovered at Naburn, near York. Excavation has uncovered the remains of circular houses up to 15 metres in diameter. They are within subrectangular ditched enclosures and surrounded by fields.

Most of the evidence for the wealthier Brigantes comes from Stanwick, a defended site of about 760 acres which is surrounded by a ditch and a stone-revetted bank, with gates at the entrance. Located where the northern route east of the Pennines meets the Stainmore Pass, the stronghold may possibly have been the headquarters of Queen Cartimandua or another important leader. There is evidence of much activity at the site soon after the Roman invasion of Britain. Roman goods began to arrive in the 40s, including pottery imported from France and glass bowls from Italy. Roofing tiles of Roman type have also been found, suggesting the presence of at least one Romanised building.

The wealth of the Stanwick community is also seen in a hoard of decorated metalwork found outside the earthworks. The hoard includes chariot fittings, harness mounts and a sword scabbard. These items will have been made for tribal leaders and show both their taste, and the skill of the Brigantian metalworkers. One of the most interesting discoveries at Stanwick was made during the excavation of the ditch at one of the gates. A sword was found still in its scabbard, and close to it was a human skull with severe head wounds. These may have been part of a trophy hung at the gate.

Pre-Roman craftsman with metalworker's tongs

4

Reconstruction of native house at Naburn

Bronze head of Brigantian horned god, from Aldborough

5

A PROFESSIONAL ARMY
Legions and Auxiliaries

The Roman army of the 1st and 2nd centuries was one of the most professional fighting forces to exist until modern times. Its soldiers served for 25 years and were highly trained in the use of weapons, in route marching, swimming and cavalry manoeuvres. The army first emerged as a permanent force in the 1st century B.C. when it conquered Western Europe. At the time when it came to Britain, it was composed of 28 legions and accompanying auxiliary forces, a total manpower of about 300,000 men. The units were dispersed over the Empire, mainly in areas where they could guard frontiers and police newly won territories.

The legions were the prestigious, heavily armed infantry units, reserved for Roman citizens. They each had about 5,300 men, sub-divided into fighting units of 480 men, known as cohorts. They were trained to use javelins and swords in battle and had spring-guns known as *ballistae* which fired iron bolts and were sometimes mounted on carriages drawn by mules.

The auxiliary units were recruited from non-citizens in the frontier provinces. They were grouped into regiments of light infantry, cavalry, or mixed units of between 500 and 1,000 strong. They were well-trained and dedicated soldiers whose function in battle was to attack the enemy, the legionaries being kept in reserve and used only if necessary. Unlike the legionaries, who wore heavy armour, the auxiliaries usually had leather jerkins. Sometimes they wore light scale armour or chainmail which allowed greater mobility in battle. The infantry normally carried swords and the cavalry used both slashing swords and lances. Some auxiliaries were armed with less conventional weapons. These units included Hamian archers from Syria and spearman from Raetia, both stationed in Britain.

The legions undertook a full range of activities beyond those of training, parading, fighting and frontier control. These included farming,

Roman legionaries in battle with *ballistae* from Trajan's column

mining, manufacture of weapons and armour, and construction of roads, bridges and buildings. Within the legions there were soldiers who were architects, engineers and surveyors and others who were specialised craftsmen such as carpenters, masons, plumbers, glaziers, potters, blacksmiths and leatherworkers. Those men who did not have particular skills provided the general workforce. We know a lot about day to day life in the army from historians' accounts, official military documents and soldiers' letters. One of the documents to survive on papyrus is part of a duty roster for the 3rd legion, for ten days in October 87. One of the soldiers listed on the roster was sent to work in the armoury, the quarries, the baths and on the artillery, as well as to do general military duty on different days in that period.

The organisation and technical skills of the legions had a profound influence on the lives of the local Britons. Never before had there been roads carefully routed, constructed, and drained to give maximum ease and efficiency of transport. The Roman engineers designed bridges which could span rivers of great width and depth. The masonry and timber buildings were not only of sound, squared construction, but often monumental in scale, with columns and other features of classical architecture. These contrasted greatly with the simple, round houses inhabited by the Britons. Since the Britons did not know how to build in Roman style, army architects and legionaries were probably seconded to help local authorities with their building programmes.

In this country most Roman buildings have been long dismantled and their stones reused for other buildings. Buried Roman roads can still be traced over the British landscape, many largely underlying our existing roads. In most instances the evidence for Roman structures comes from aerial photographs which record buried features as marks in crops and also from archaeological excavation. However, there are remains of some Roman structures that survive above ground as monuments to their greatness. The most impressive are Hadrian's Wall and parts of the fortress walls at York and Chester.

Roman road known as Wade's Causeway on the North Yorkshire Moors

GARRISONS AND FRONTIERS

Roman forts and fortresses conformed in their planning to basic principles but were far from identical in detail. They were normally rectangular in shape and were defended either by a turf rampart or a stone wall backed by an earth bank and had single or multiple ditches. Towers were set at intervals along the defensive circuit and at the gateways. The internal layout was divided by a rectangular grid of streets, the main roads leading to the gates. The headquarters building was placed centrally, with officers' accommodation, barracks, granaries, hospital, stables and workshops fitted tightly into the surrounding areas.

Five different periods of construction of the defences of the York fortress have been noted in excavation. The inscription from King's Square records the rebuilding in stone of the south-east gate of the fortress during the reign of the Emperor Trajan in 107-8. Part of the colonnaded hall of the headquarters building has been excavated beneath York Minster. Built in the early 2nd century, it had administrative offices and the shrine housing the standards of the legion opening off the aisled hall. Below it was a cellar serving as the treasury for the soldiers' pay. Little is known about other internal buildings of the York fortress, though some barracks have been located, as well as part of the bath-house.

The map of the northern military sites shows how the auxiliary forts relate to the frontier and to the fortress at York. The Emperor Hadrian had the frontier, known as Hadrian's Wall, built between the Tyne and Solway Firth in the years 122-125. It consisted of a continuous wall or turf bank, with towers and fortlets at regular intervals along its length. Auxiliary forts were added later. It was used as the frontier except for a brief period when another barrier, between the Forth and the Clyde, was established in 143 and occupied for about 20 years. Known as the Antonine Wall, it was of turf construction with closely spaced forts set along its length. The auxiliary forts behind the frontier lines were occupied, on and off, depending on the military

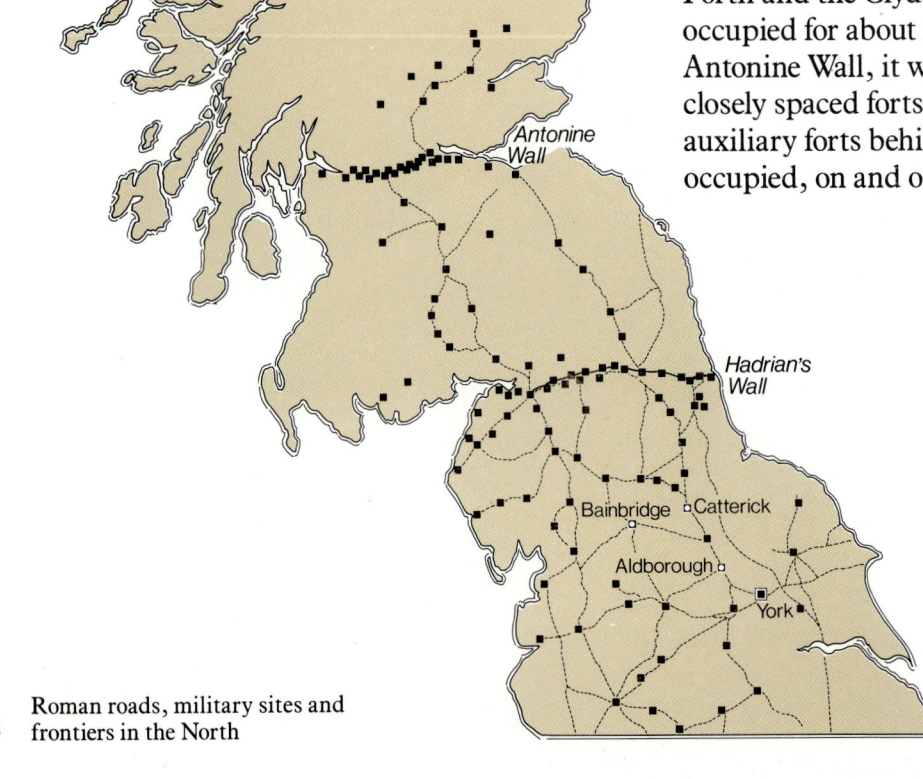

Roman roads, military sites and frontiers in the North

needs of the time, but the legionary fortress at York was permanently held as the headquarters for the North throughout the Roman occupation. Its garrison was the 9th legion, replaced in about 122 by the 6th legion.

Gate inscription from York fortress recording the construction of the gate in 107-8. The inscription when complete would have been:

> 'The Emperor Caesar Nerva Trajan Augustus, son of the deified Nerva, Conqueror of Germany, Conqueror of Dacia, *pontifex maximus;* in his twelfth year of tribunician power, six times acclaimed *imperator;* five times *consul;* father of his country, built this gate by the agency of the 9th Legion Hispana.'

The auxiliary fort at Housesteads on Hadrian's Wall

LINKS WITH ROME
Emperors in Britain

P. Aelius Hadrianus
Emperor 117-138

Hadrian was born in 76 in the Roman *colonia* at Italica in southern Spain of an old Roman family. He became the ward of his cousin, the Emperor Trajan, and eventually succeeded him.

In his youth he served as a staff officer in legions stationed on the Danube and Rhine. Later he commanded a legion in the second Dacian war in 105 and governed Pannonia and then Syria. At this time he must have seen for himself how barbarian pressure was increasing around the fringes of the Empire.

When he became Emperor, he was the first to build frontier barriers in the provinces. He also tightened up military discipline in the frontier areas. He undertook extensive tours of the Empire, including one to Britain in 122. Hadrian's biographer records that when he came to Britain 'he put many things right and was the first to build a wall 80 miles long to separate Romans and barbarians.' Matters which he attended to in Britain included the draining of the Fenland of East Anglia and Lincolnshire, and the promotion of Romanisation in some of the towns in the Midlands. He was probably responsible for the development of Aldborough as the Brigantian centre and he no doubt encouraged urbanisation at York.

But Hadrian was far from being only a military man. His interests extended to music, the arts, and particularly to architecture. He wrote poetry, and his poem on his approaching death is regarded as a classic.

'Little tender wand'ring soul,
Body's guest and comrade thou,
To what bourne, all bare and pale,
Wilt thou be a' faring now,
All the merry jest and play
Thou so lovest put away?'

L. Septimius Severus
Emperor 193-211

Severus was born in 146 at Leptis Magna, a flourishing town in Tripolitania. After administrative experience in Sardinia, Spain and France he was governing Pannonia when the death of the Emperor Commodus, late in 192, led to a period of chaos. Although he was proclaimed Emperor in 193 by his own troops, and soon gained control of Rome, he had two major rivals. The governors of Syria and Britain, both with powerful armies, made bids for the Empire, and it was only in 197 that Severus finally secured his position.

Severus was a ruthless, ambitious man and a careful planner. Since Severus realised that his power relied on the support of the army, he allowed the troops privileges, such as the right to marry while serving. His wife was given the title 'Mother of the Army.' As a precautionary measure against rebellion he split some provinces, such as Britain, into smaller units with fewer troops.

In 208 Severus came to Britain to fight against the Caledonian tribes of northern Scotland. His biographers hint that one reason was to get his two sons away from the luxuries and pleasures of

Rome. When he was not campaigning, he and his wife probably lived at York with their sons. He died in York in February 211. He was cremated and his ashes were taken back to Rome in an urn said variously to have been of gold, porphyry or alabaster.

Flavius Valerius Constantinus
Emperor 306-337

Constantine the Great was born at Naïssus in modern Yugoslavia in about 274. He was the son of Constantius Chlorus, who became a Caesar in 293. Constantine's abilities were spotted early. When his father was campaigning in Britain, Constantine was sent out to help him. His father died in York on 25 June, 306 and Constantine was proclaimed Emperor here by the troops. Thereafter he had a long struggle to eliminate rivals until eventually he became sole ruler of the Empire in 323. He was a brilliantly outstanding general who believed firmly in his own destiny. He was a talented administrator who ranks with Diocletian as the restorer of the Empire.

Constantine's mother, Helena, was a Christian and he adopted the faith although he was only baptised when he was dying. In 313 Constantine and his co-emperor issued an Edict stating that they were granting full tolerance to Christianity as to all other religions. Thereby the importance of the Church was established during his reign.

THE EMERGENCE OF TOWNS

Soon after the Roman invasion, traders and others began to settle outside forts and to acquire Roman customs. We know from Tacitus that the Romans also set out 'to show the Britons the Roman way of life.' The Britons were encouraged to build towns and to use as their model the *colonia* at Colchester, built by the legionary veterans themselves. Based on standard Roman planning, these towns had straight streets intersecting at right angles, well-designed drainage and public water-supply systems, colonnaded porticos and impressive public buildings such as forums and basilicas, baths and temples. The larger towns also had theatres and amphitheatres.

Urbanism was something new to the Britons and despite the growth of the towns only a small percentage of the population accepted city life. Most continued to have their roots in the countryside. This was true of the Brigantes.

In the north two principal towns developed, Aldborough and York. Aldborough, Isurium Brigantum, built soon after 120, was the administrative centre for the Brigantes and the principal market town. Here a tribal council composed of the Brigantian aristocracy met to run the judicial system, to look after public buildings and roads, and to collect local taxes. We do not know much about the town archaeologically since the site has not been threatened by modern development and only limited excavation has taken place. It was enclosed by ditches and banks in the mid 2nd century and given a stone wall in the 3rd century.

The settlement at York, Eburacum, on the south side of the River Ouse, grew from a trading community into a self-governing town before the beginning of the 3rd century. It became the provincial capital of Lower Britain in the early 3rd century and was probably made a *colonia* about the same time. Its council, a mixture of prosperous locals and legionary veterans, governed only the town. Little is known about the buildings in the *colonia*, because the modern town overlies the deeply buried Roman deposits and excavation is difficult.

There were a number of smaller towns in the north serving as market centres. One which has been extensively excavated is at Catterick, Cataractonium, which started off as a small settlement outside a fort, at the crossing of the River Swale. In the 2nd century, a public posting station or *mansio* was built along the main road north. The posting station had rooms for official travellers and its own bath-suite. In the courtyard outside the entrance stood a Jupiter column. Across the road were shops and other buildings, including a temple. The town was walled in the late 3rd century.

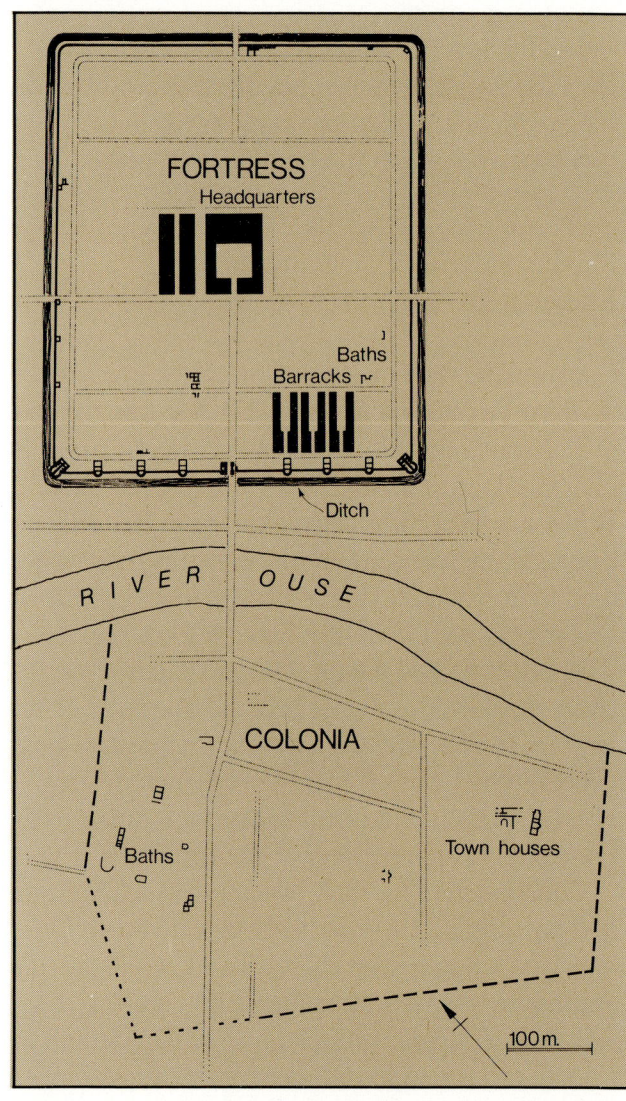

Plan of Roman York

Reconstruction of the *mansio* at Catterick with the bath block on the right and the sleeping accommodation at the back

Pottery cult mask found near a temple, from Catterick

13

URBAN LIFE

York became one of the most important towns in Britain, second only to London. Since it was an international port as well, it had a cosmopolitan mixture of people from all over the Empire. We know the names and origins of some of the wealthier people of York from inscriptions on stone. One of those mentioned is Verecundius Diogenes who came from Bourges in France and was an official of the organisation responsible for the Imperial Cult in York. His wife, Julia Fortunata, came from Sardinia. Another was L. Viducius Placidus, a merchant from the Rouen area. Such merchants and members of the town council had a luxurious lifestyle and large staffs of servants. The poorer classes in York, such as craftsmen and shopkeepers, were very much part of the thriving community and on the whole enjoyed a comfortable standard of living.

Many of the inhabitants, including some artisans, could read and write. Formal education was available to the wealthy. Tacitus tells us that when Agricola became governor 'he began to educate the sons of nobles in the liberal arts... And those who previously refused to use Latin began to wish for fluency in it.' One of the teachers used by Agricola was Demetrius Scribonius who, when he came to York, made two religious dedications in Greek.

Those who could afford it, often wished to have classical decoration such as painted wall plaster and mosaic flooring in their homes. Most had a liking for Roman food and drink. Large quantities of wine were drunk and food was cooked in oil and highly seasoned.

The commercial and administrative heart of the town was the forum which included a colonnaded market square, a basilica used for law courts and meetings of the council, and the town offices.

The social centre of the town was the public baths where people exchanged news, gossiped and played board games as well as bathed. The bathers cleaned their bodies by sweating in heated rooms. Attendants then scraped, massaged and oiled their skins. They could also wash themselves in the cold and hot plunge baths opening off the main rooms. Those who wished could exercise and play games in a courtyard or hall which was part of the baths.

The Roman custom of holding public entertainment in towns soon caught on. Gladiator fights, acrobatic shows and beast hunts were held in amphitheatres, and plays were performed in outdoor theatres. Chariot races were popular. People from the surrounding countryside flocked to see the shows.

Marble figure of an athlete wearing a victor's laurel wreath, from York

Enamelled perfume flask, bronze oil container and suspension chain

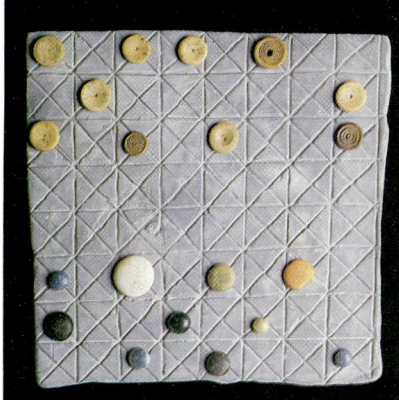

Mock gaming board with antler, bone and glass counters

Reconstruction of a Roman kitchen

HOUSES
Design and decoration

There were great differences between the pre-Roman house in Britain and the simplest Romanised house. The pre-Roman house was usually round, without a proper floor and open in plan. Even the simplest houses of Roman type had a rectangular shell, and were divided into rooms used for particular purposes. Recent evidence suggests that more houses had upper floors than was once thought.

Looking at details of finish, the Roman house had tile or slate roofing, glazed windows, fitted doors with locks, and often mortar or stone floors. Verandahs with roofs supported on stone columns were common, and both external and internal walls were plastered. The inside walls were normally painted. Some houses had walls and ceilings decorated in styles used at Pompeii. The popular designs included imitation panelling and architectural perspectives. Most houses were heated by charcoal braziers, but the larger ones had several rooms with an under-floor heating system, known as the hypocaust.

The main room of larger houses was the *triclinium*, or dining room. At one end of the room there was often a semi-circular apse, used as the dining area. Here the main meal of the day was eaten, the diners reclining on couches around small tables. This room and the other principal rooms of the house, usually had wall paintings and a mosaic floor.

Mosaics came into common use in the 2nd century. The designs, which were probably taken from pattern books, included geometric patterns, animals, fishes and Graeco-Roman mythological subjects. Aldborough has produced many mosaics, one of which has the Muses and a simple Greek inscription telling us that they are on Mount Helicon. Mosaics have also been found at York and at villas in the area, and it seems there was a firm of mosaicists working at York or Aldborough in the late 3rd century.

Room of a house with wall paintings similar to that from Catterick

The Four Seasons mosaic from Toft Green, York

DRESS AND FASHION

Our knowledge of what the people in Roman Britain wore comes largely from tombstones, since their garments have mainly disintegrated in the ground. However, waterlogged or peaty soil has sometimes preserved textile garments and leather footwear.

There was a remarkable discovery on Grewelthorpe Moor near Ripon in the 19th century when the body of a man was found in the peat. It is said that he was dressed in a green cloak, scarlet tunic and yellow stockings and it was thought at the time that he was a Romano-Briton. Unfortunately, all that was kept was the sole of one of his boots and part of a stocking, not enough to establish the date conclusively as Roman.

At York there are a number of gravestones which show individuals who lived in the town. The tombstone of Flavia Augustina is particularly important since it shows a family in Roman provincial dress. Augustina is seen wearing a full length tunic which hangs in deep folds to her ankles. She also has a cloak thrown back over her shoulders. Her husband is wearing a similar tunic of shorter length and over it he has a hooded cape. The two young boys are dressed in outfits similar to their father's. This was the standard dress of the well-to-do in Britain throughout most of the Roman period.

Woman wearing a long tunic and cloak standing with her son. Behind, is a man wearing a tunic, standard Roman dress

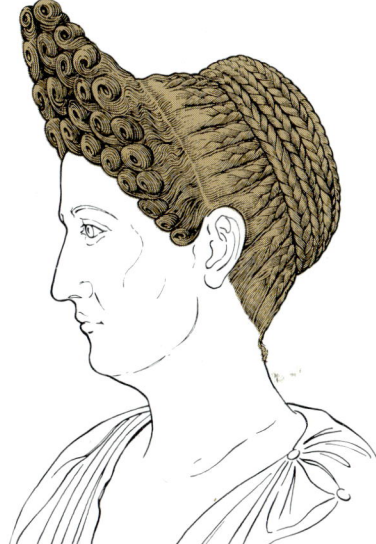

Hairstyle, late 1st century

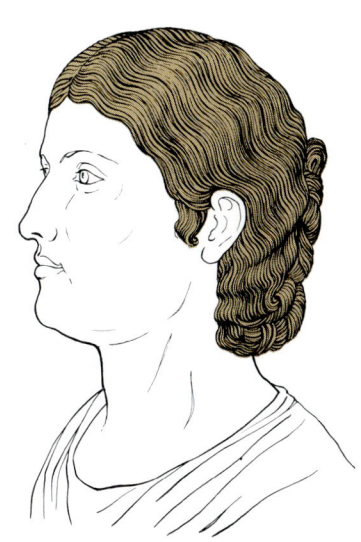

Hairstyle, mid to late 2nd century

Hairstyle, late 2nd – early 3rd century

17

In the 3rd and 4th centuries a semi-circular cape, which was fastened by a large brooch on the right shoulder, came into fashion. These are seen on two of the portrait medallions from York carved in jet.

Tunics were worn by all classes of society but those of the servants had long sleeves and less body width to give ease of movement. They were shaped differently for manual work. The blacksmith on the tombstone from York is wearing a short, belted tunic fastened only on the left shoulder, leaving the right arm free. A native style of tunic which continued to be worn by some women had the overtunic pinned by brooches at the shoulders.

What is striking is the lack of representations in Britain of people wearing togas, the Roman ceremonial dress. This is presumably because they were worn only on formal occasions by high Roman officials.

Provincial dress scarcely altered over a period of more than 400 years but fashions in hairstyles changed rapidly. The fashions were set by ladies at the court and keenly followed by women all over the Empire. Well-to-do women had maids to arrange their hair for them. Several styles are shown on the stone sculptures and jet pendants from York. But most striking of all is the auburn hair of a young girl, held in a bun by two jet pins, found in a late Roman grave.

Official of the 1st century wearing a toga

Lady and her attendants

Jet pendant from York with the portraits of a husband and wife

RURAL LIFE
Farmsteads and villas

The Romans had little effect on the lifestyle of the Brigantes who lived in the countryside. Much of northern Britain being hilly with thin, moorland soils, was not suitable for growing cereal crops. The people in these areas were mainly pastoralists, depending on cattle and sheep for their living. They would have sold hides and wool in the local market centres in exchange for Roman coins and manufactured goods. Most of the profits will have gone to middle men and the farmers did not have the money to Romanize their farms even if they wanted to.

Those farmers who lived in the lowland areas where mixed farming was usually profitable often enlarged their farms and replaced their round houses by stone rectangular buildings of Roman type. These Romanized farms are known as villas. The main house of a villa resembled a town house in having hypocaust systems for heating, mosaic floors, decorated walls and sometimes a private bath-suite. Most of the villas also had separate bath houses for the estate workers and their families. Barns and other farm buildings were located near the house and during the 3rd and 4th centuries when villas became more prosperous, additional houses were usually provided for family or farm managers.

An example of a villa which has been extensively excavated is the one at Gargrave, near Skipton. In the 3rd century is had a principal house with bath-suite, a separate bath house,

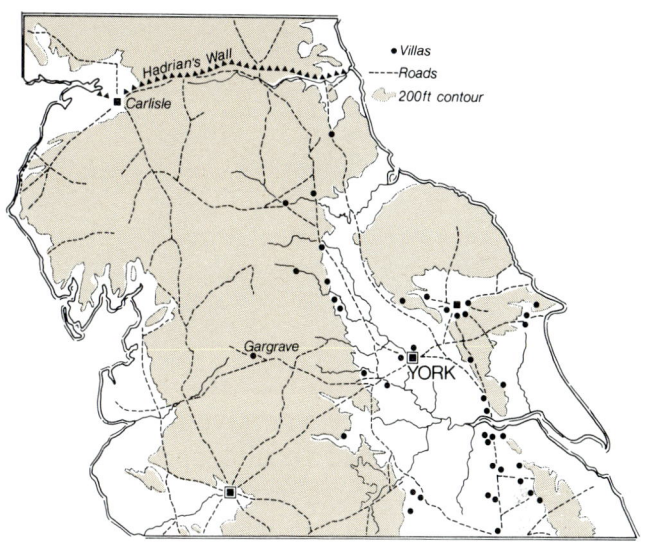

Villas in the North which would have been greatly outnumbered by native farmsteads

two additional dwellings and farm office all within the central enclosure. The field system of the villa is visible on the ground but is only fully understood from the air. Some of the fields are long and narrow, designed for the use of a heavy plough.

Improvements in stock and agriculture were introduced during the Roman period. New breeds of cattle appeared as well as the white-fleeced woolly sheep. An important innovation was the two handed scythe which meant that larger quantities of hay could be mowed quickly and stored for winter feed.

Reconstruction of a harvesting machine

In about the 3rd century, a new type of plough came into use which had a coulter and perhaps a mould board. This plough was able to cultivate the heavier, more fertile soils which increased the profits of the farmers. Simple harvesting machines were probably used by this time.

Large areas of the villa estates were devoted to growing trees since timber was in constant demand. Wood was used for cooking and heating and was sold for the construction of buildings, ships and carts. To provide one small bath house with fuel required 23 hectares of woodland which would be coppiced.

The villa at Gargrave in the 3rd century

A bronze figurine of a Romano-British ploughman and his team from Piercebridge, Co. Durham

Brooches in the shape of a lion, hare and cockerel

COMMERCE
Merchants and Craftsmen

The Roman way of life depended on being able to obtain a wide range of reasonably priced goods and commodities, some of which were imported from great distances. Goods were produced in bulk and transported efficiently over land and sea. The easy movement of goods was possible because of the excellent roads and well-designed, efficient ports. To keep the cost down, wherever possible transport was by river rather than by road since it was quicker and ships could take larger loads. The wholesale trade was handled by merchants like Marcus Aurelius Lunaris who operated from York and Lincoln and traded with Bordeaux. He dedicated an altar at Bordeaux in 237 on which he mentioned his links with the *coloniae* at York and Lincoln.

Most trade in the Roman Empire was in agricultural products and raw materials. Those imported into Britain were wine, olive oil, fish sauces, figs, grapes and olives. Britain exported hides, wool, metals, hunting dogs, pearls and oysters, and also grain in the late Roman period. As far as is known Britain exported few finished goods though textiles were almost certainly exported, in particular British cloaks.

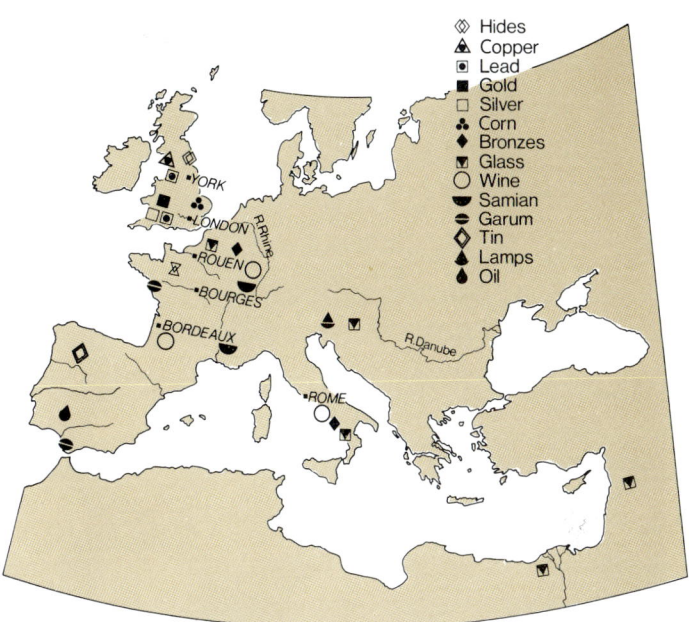

Trade between Britain and the Continent with areas of origin of the main products marked

Jet jewellery from the York factory and souvenir vessels of Hadrian's Wall have been found on the Continent. Among the imports to Britain were fine glassware, samian tableware, metal vessels, marble veneers and statuary.

Stone monument in the shape of a ship carrying barrels of wine

Bronze steelyard with weight and 1st-century silver coins

Many commodities were transported in standardized containers which could be packed closely together on ships and carts. Pottery and glass containers were normally packed in straw to prevent breakage. Barrels travelled without extra protection.

The first two centuries saw a large volume of imports into Britain from the Continent. By the 3rd century the level of imports decreased considerably because Britain was becoming more self-sufficient in manufactured goods and the production of goods on the Continent was declining because of adverse political conditions. Britain had a more favourable balance of trade and gradually became more prosperous.

In Britain most goods were manufactured within the country, not imported. Items were mainly produced in small workshops, often with living quarters adjoining. Many of these workshops faced onto the main streets of the towns. Among the activities which took place were leatherworking, joinery, smithing, weaving, dyeing, brewing, bone working and basketry. The goods were normally sold on the premises.

Certain industries were kept outside the towns because they produced fumes or were a fire risk. Among these were smelting, potting, tanning and charcoal burning.

The craftsmen were mainly Britons who soon produced goods of standard Roman type and design. However, certain types of metalwork, particularly brooches and dress fasteners, were made in the North in styles inspired by native tradition. Among those were dragonesque and trumpet brooches. The British were skilled in the use of enamels and continued to decorate their bronzes with them.

In York there is evidence for smithing and the manufacture of jet objects, pottery and tiles. From Norton an inscribed stone records a goldsmith's workshop run by a young slave. At Catterick evidence of leatherworking was found outside the fort. Many shops have been excavated in the later town, among them a bronze-smith's workshop of the late 3rd and 4th centuries.

Fishing was an important industry since fish was eaten regularly and used for making the sauces which accompanied many Roman dishes. York has produced evidence for manufacture of fish sauces in the 4th century.

DEATH AND BURIAL
Cemeteries at York

In immediately pre-Roman times many Britons were exceedingly casual about disposal of their dead. Skeletons were sometimes thrown into rubbish pits. In contrast the Romans were always anxious for decent burial and some of them even had tombstones made for themselves during their lifetime. There were organisations which they could join which were devoted to ensuring proper burial for their members and which provided funeral banquets for their survivors. They believed in a more-or-less shadowy life after death in which the spirits of the deceased could not rest unless the correct rituals had been performed.

Since Roman law forbade burial in built-up areas, the cemeteries were usually along the main roads leading from the settlements. In the early Roman period most bodies were cremated. The ashes were usually interred in pots, glass vessels or lead containers. One lead cremation urn from York has a hole in its lid for the insertion of a pipe down which libations will have been poured from the surface.

By the later second century, inhumations with or without coffins became increasingly common. Wealthy citizens sometimes had tombs built above ground in which their stone coffins were placed. Their coffins were often carved and inscribed since they were meant to be seen. At a slightly lower level of society burials were marked on the surface by elaborately carved tombstones such as Julia Velva's. The burials often had rich grave-goods, including jewellery and glass vessels as well as pots.

Just off the road to Tadcaster, at Trentholme Drive, was a cemetery for the poor of the *colonia*. It was carefully excavated in the 1950s. Most of the burials had meagre grave-goods,

Bronze statuette of the god Vulcan, from Catterick

Pot in the form of a female head, York

usually only pots. Examination of the bones showed that the average age at death for those surviving infancy was about 40. Most interesting of all is the fact that womens' skeletons tended to be similar, but the mens' were much more varied and included some with Near Eastern and African characteristics.

The burials north of the river will have been mainly those of soldiers and their dependents. One especially interesting one has a Christian motto carved in bone. In the 4th century York had numerous burials in which gypsum was poured into the coffins, evidently with the hope of preserving the bodies. These burials are thought to be Christian.

Burials from cemetery at Trentholme Drive, York

Grave goods from female burial, Sycamore Place, York, including a bone plaque with a Christian inscription

RELIGION
Cults and temples

In Roman Britain there was a great mixture of religions. Some were initially purely native, often becoming partly Romanised, some were completely Roman and others were exotic cults brought to Britain by merchants or soldiers from far-flung parts of the Empire. All these cults had temples or shrines as well as their priests and altars. In most cults animals were sacrificed and incense was burnt at altars. Small altars dedicated by individuals were often placed inside temples. The main altars, which were larger, were often placed outside, since most temples were too small for big ceremonies.

All military units and civic authorities were expected to join in the formal worship of Iuppiter Optimus Maximus as State God, or in the Imperial Cult, which involved ceremonies in honour of the Emperors and their families. Private individuals were allowed complete freedom of religion so long as they were prepared to take part in the Imperial Cult.

The Britons worshipped many nature gods, particularly those of rivers and springs. They also had many deities concerned with war, healing, fertility, and the sky. Such cults were given distinctive temples which usually had a square sanctuary towering above a surrounding colonnaded verandah. Where their dedications are known, the native god or goddess is usually equated with one or more Roman deities. For instance, Nodens, a Celtic healing god is sometimes identified with Mars, the war god, or sometimes with Silvanus, god of the wild. Occasionally, as with the cult of Sulis Minerva at Bath, a temple was built in Graeco-Roman style, on a platform with columns supporting a triangular pediment. But temples of this type were distinctly rare in Britain.

Troops sent to Britain from other provinces often continued to worship their own deities. For instance, the cult of the Mother Goddesses, popular in the Rhineland, appears particularly in the military areas of Britain. The dedication of a temple to the Egyptian god Serapis by a legionary commander at York is a reminder that eastern cults often attracted officers and merchants. York has also produced evidence for Mithraism, originally a Persian religion which became particularly popular with Roman officers. Because of its high moral principles this cult was a rival of Christianity.

There will have been some individual Christians in Britain in the early Roman period, but there is no sign of an organised church before Constantine. In 314 the Bishop of York attended a council at Arles with other British

A Romano-British temple

Christ's head and Chi Rho monogram from a mosaic at Hinton St Mary, Dorset

bishops. His cathedral would probably have been in the *colonia*, but apart from some likely Christian burials, archaeology has not yet produced evidence for the Christian community at York.

A TIME OF CHANGE
The 4th century

In the late 3rd and 4th centuries much of the administration of the Empire was reorganised by Diocletian and Constantine the Great. Britain was then split into four provinces, one of which continued to be ruled from York. Reform of the army made the legions smaller and less important, with greater emphasis on the use of cavalry. New forts, designed to take mobile units, were built on the main road north. York became the headquarters of the Dux Britanniarum, commander of the forces stationed on Hadrian's Wall and in some of the forts to the rear. The river frontage of the York fortress was rebuilt and given massive towers, which made it one of the most impressive fortifications in the Empire.

A late Roman document, known as the *Notitia Dignitatum*, lists all the civil and military posts as well as the military units in the North. It shows that many regiments were recruited from barbarian, particularly Germanic, tribes from outside the empire. This led to new styles of military dress and equipment. The troops wore belts with fittings and buckles inspired by Germanic types. Short javelins were now carried as well as the standard sword and spears. The cavalrymen and their horses were often heavily armoured and both stirrups and spurs came into use.

In the disturbed period towards the end of the 4th century some towns in Britain had military units in garrison. At Catterick a late 4th-century compound with an arched entrance was created in the middle of the town by extensively altering existing buildings. This compound almost certainly housed an army unit, as late military equipment was found there and in the vicinity. By 410 the army had been totally withdrawn, and the native communities were left to defend themselves, gradually becoming less and less Roman.

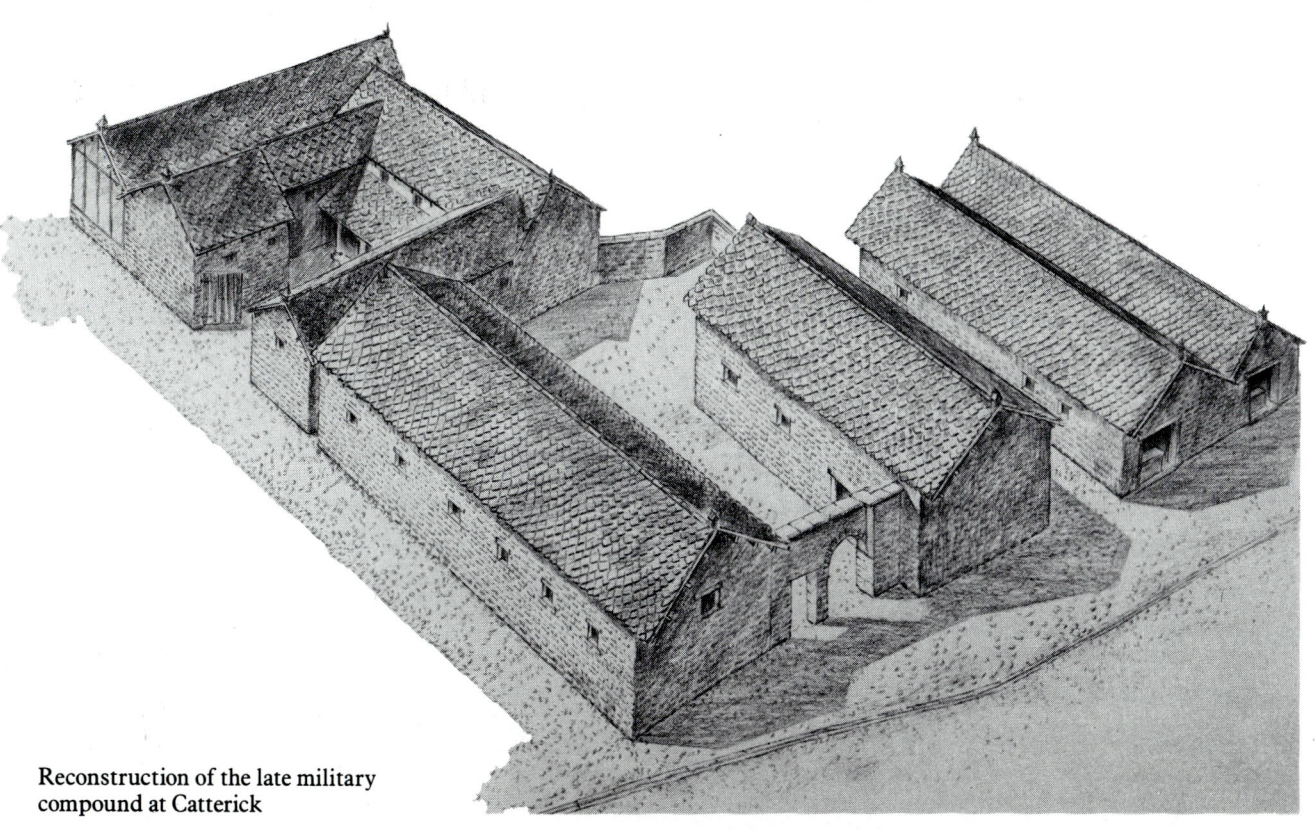

Reconstruction of the late military compound at Catterick

Reconstruction of river front of the York fortress in the 4th century

The corner tower of the York defences in the Museum Gardens